Glen Folk Village

A Padraig Bear Adventure

Maria A. Mannion

Padraig Bear

Dedicated to the memory of my father
Henry Joseph Savage (1927-2009),
without whom this story would not have been
possible.

For Paige, Lee and Callum with love
Grammie xx

Acknowledgements:

Margaret Rose Cunningham and the staff at Glen Folk Village, Glencolmcille, Co. Donegal, Ireland.

Glen Folk Village

Padraig was a bear. Not just any bear but a travelling bear and a story telling bear. He loved nothing more than listening to people and their tales. He wondered what he would discover at Glen Folk Village.

He opened the door of a cottage and was amazed at what he saw! There was an open fire with peat logs surrounded by lots of three legged black pots. Some were small and some were very big, but they all looked very heavy!

"Oh, a spinning wheel! I've always wanted to try one of these. Yikes, the wool is getting caught in my paws!"

Padraig spoke out loud as he thought he was alone.

Who could that be?

"Hi, I'm Rosie. I'm in charge of this cottage."

Sitting on the bed beside the fire was a lovely doll, with beautiful red hair. Padraig hurried over to apologise for he wanted to make a new friend.

"Have you any stories about spinning wheels?" he asked.

"Plenty," Rosie replied, "but first tidy up the mess you made, the fairies don't like it!"

Rosie explained that during the night the fairies came and did spinning. Padraig hurried to tidy up – he definitely did not want to annoy fairies!

"That's Mary in the photograph on the wall. She uses that spinning wheel all the time."

"When she has spun the wool, she makes socks and garments to keep her family warm. She gets her wool from the sheep that she keeps on the hills nearby."

"She sings songs while she spins – my favourite is called "The Spinning Wheel". It really sounds like the movement of the wheel."

"Sometimes lots of people come together and they have a spinning, weaving and knitting evening!

"I think I'll try some sewing instead," said Padraig making his way over to a lovely treadle sewing machine.

Padraig got himself settled on a chair and then discovered a problem – his legs were too short to reach the treadle! Rosie had to laugh!

"Mary loves her sewing machine. Her son Sean emigrated to America to find work because there is very little work here, and when he had saved enough money he told his mother to buy one of these new machines. It is so much quicker than sewing by hand. Mary wastes nothing and even small pieces of material can be made into patchwork covers just like the one on the bed."

"You do know a lot of stories, Rosie. I'm really glad I met you", said Padraig.

Did you know?

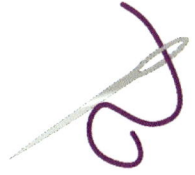

The first working sewing machine was made in France in 1830! On August 12th 1851 Isaac Singer, an American, patented the first practical and efficient sewing machine. The name "Singer" has become associated with sewing machines the world over.

Padraig was eager to find something he could do, not having had much luck with the spinning wheel and the sewing machine.

"Now, this looks interesting. I wonder what it does?" Padraig inspected it carefully. It was a barrel with a handle – just waiting to be turned!

"Be careful, Padraig, sometimes that butter churn takes on a life of its own," Rosie warned.

Butter churn? But the warning came too late.......

..... the speed of the turning handle lifted Padraig into the air and sent him flying across the room landing in a bag on the coat rack with a little hat on his head!

Just then the door opened and in came a lady who looked in astonishment at the little bear caught in a bag!

"Maggie, this is Padraig come to visit, but he is not having much luck helping out," explained Rosie.

She told Maggie that Padraig had got the spinning yarn caught in his paws, his legs were not long enough to work the sewing machine and he wasn't heavy enough to turn the butter churn!

"Looks like that leprechaun in the butter churn took a disliking to you, little Padraig Bear, but not to worry, you'll be alright when you get a wee cup of tea in you," said Maggie.

She lifted Padraig carefully from the bag giving him a little cuddle before setting him down.

Did you know?

If you shake cream in a jar with a tight lid for a long time you can make butter. If you half fill a butter churn barrel, then flip it over and over, you may get the job done in half an hour. About 40 turns every minute is said to be a good rate for best results. Check through the glass peephole in the lid and see if the butter is ready.

Well, Padraig was delighted to hear that, as he was beginning to feel a little hungry. He had been through so much since breakfast. As quick as a flash he jumped up onto a seat at the table. Boiled eggs his favourite!

Maggie and Rosie both started to laugh!

"Padraig Bear," said Maggie, "this is a working kitchen. If you want some tea here you have to help make it."

Padraig got down off the chair and hurried over to the hearth for he was eager to help. He looked at all the pots and kettles carefully. He didn't think he could lift any of them, they had to be heavy.

Rosie saw Padraig looking at the pots and she explained that all the cooking was done over the turf fire with the pots.

"The big pots are used for boiling potatoes and 'pot luck' stews. The griddles are used for baking bread. To wash down the potatoes at a meal there will be lots and lots of buttermilk."

"Come outside and see the even bigger pot, Padraig," Rosie continued. "It was used in Famine Times when the potatoes were bad. The government supplied the pots and made soup to feed the hungry people. The pot is kept here to remind us of that terrible time when 1 million people died and 1 million people left Ireland."

Rosie and Padraig stood in silence for a minute and said a quiet prayer.

Did you know?

Around 1570 Sir Walter Raleigh brought the potato to Ireland from The New World. It became a staple food for many Irish people. 225 years later it was the cause of one of the most tragic events in Irish history, The Great Hunger of 1845 – 1848.

When Padraig stepped back into the room, the peat fire was burning bright, the tea was ready and lots more people had arrived.

"Goodness me," said Padraig, "this is turning out to be quite a party!"

"Padraig, here's something you CAN do!" said Rosie. "Can you make the cross on the top of the soda farl before we cook it – it helps to keep the devil away and protects the whole household!"

Finally it was time to eat and Padraig had second helpings!

The craic lasted so long that Padraig fell asleep in the arms of another visitor! He knew he had to go home but he would be back.

Padraig's postcard from

Glencolmcille

Padraig was sure there were many more stories to find here.

That was for another day...

ACTIVITIES

Music

The Spinning Wheel

Music and Lyrics

Padraig learnt to sing this song, can you?

The Spinning Wheel

"Eileen, *a chara*, I hear someone tapping"
"'Tis the ivy dear mother against the glass flapping"
"Eily, I surely hear somebody sighing"
"'Tis the sound mother dear of the autumn winds dying."

"What's the noise that I hear at the window I wonder"
"'Tis the little birds chirping, the holly-bush under"
"What makes you be shoving and moving your stool on
And singing all wrong the old song of 'The Coolin'?"

There's a form at the casement, the form of her true love
And he whispers with face bent, "I'm waiting for you, love"
Get up on the stool, through the lattice step lightly
And we'll rove in the grove while the moon's shining
brightly."

The maid shakes her head, on her lips lays her fingers
Steps up from the stool, longs to go and yet lingers
A frightened glance turns to her drowsy grandmother
Puts one foot on the stool, spins the wheel with the other.

Lazily, easily, swings now the wheel round
Slowly and lowly is heard now the reel's sound
Noiseless and light to the lattice above her
The maid steps then leaps to the arms of her lover.

Slower and slower and slower the wheel rings
Lower and lower and lower the reel rings
E're the reel and the wheel stopped their ringing and
moving
Through the grove the young lovers by moonlight are
roving.

Padraig learnt the names for all the things he found at the hearth in the cottage that day. Perhaps you could learn them too.

KEY
1. Salt box
2. Crane.
3. Hake.
4. Three legged pot.
5. Griddle.
6. Tongs.
7. Toastig stick.
8. Harnenstand.
9. Wooden form.
10. Peep hole: allowed man of the house, who sat opposite, to see approaching visitors.

ABOUT THE AUTHOR

Maria Mannion was born in Belfast in 1955. Graduating in 1978 with a M.A. (Honours) from The University, Dundee, she then spent several years travelling around Europe teaching English as a Foreign Language. Returning to N. Ireland she then spent over 20 years as a secondary school English Teacher encouraging creativity and imagination. In the 90s she was involved with The Pushkin Prizes for Ireland working through schools to help develop "the child within". Hence she was delighted to assist Padraig Bear in recounting his adventures.

Printed in Great Britain
by Amazon